Selling With Builders

How Realtors®

Can Profit From

Selling Builders'

New Homes

Selling With Builders

How Realtors®
Can Profit From
Selling Builders'
New Homes

Steve Hoffacker

CAPS, MCSP, MIRM

Selling With Builders

How Realtors® Can Profit From Selling Builders' New Homes

Follow-Through® is a registered service mark of Hoffacker Associates, relating to customer contact strategies in new home sales.

Cover photo by Steve Hoffacker.

© 2011 by HOFFACKER ASSOCIATES LLC
West Palm Beach, Florida, USA

ISBN: 978-0-9843524-8-7

———

Builders need customers for their new homes. As a significant source of such customers, builders recognize what you can contribute and value your participation in their new home sales process. The more you participate in the process, the more successful you'll become. In return, more of your customers will find the homes they're looking for, and all involved will come out a winner — you, the builders, and your customers.

———

Other New Home Sales Books By Steve Hoffacker

To find additional books on new home sales written by Steve Hoffacker, visit http:stevehoffacker.com/newhome salesbooks.html.

Titles are available in print (softbound) and as Kindle eBooks, and they include:

"Making The Grade: *The A-B-C's Of Rating New Home Customers*"

"Operation Discovery: *Who, What, When, Where, & More In New Home Sales*"

"Using Your Network: *Making New Home Sales With People You Already Know*"

"Making New Friends: *Connecting With Strangers To Make More New Home Sales*"

"Universal Design For Builders: *Building & Selling Accessible, Safe & Comfortable New Homes*"

"Creating A Great First Impression: *Being An Effective New Home Sales Center Receptionist*"

Table Of Contents

Preface

Selling real estate is an exciting career!

I love it, and I want you to enjoy it as well.

I hope you've had an opportunity to discover how fulfilling it can be to help people find the home that they are looking for.

Of course, it's financially rewarding as well.

I wrote this book for Realtors® although anyone who sells residential real estate can follow the examples in this book and benefit from it.

Whether you are a broker or associate, brand new in the business (or relatively so) or a seasoned veteran, this book has been prepared expressly for you.

As you know, there are two ways to make money in residential real estate (not counting land sales and leasing) – existing homes (resales) and new homes.

If you have never worked with a builder to sell one of their new homes to any of your customers, or if you do so rather infrequently, I believe that one of the most profitable business decisions you can make is to take advantage of the income potential available through "partnering" with builders to help them sell their new homes.

You can begin by establishing some alliances in advance with key builders in your area that you would like to work with, or you can simply take a customer to a builder's model home when they are looking for such an opportunity.

Builders and their onsite sales staffs at model centers or new home communities are prepared to make presentations to interested people and are equipped to process sales on a daily basis.

They welcome and look forward to your participation in the new home sales process.

They recognize you as a significant source of potential buyers for their new homes and as an important influence upon those customers that you take to see and consider their homes.

It is a win-win-win business relationship because you make money for producing a sale, builders make money by selling their homes, and your customers obtain their new homes.

If you already have been working with builders to help them sell their new homes and help your customers find what they're looking for, that's great.

If not, I urge you to consider the career opportunities and financial advantage from doing so.

If you already have experiences in showing and selling new homes, this book will serve as a refresher for you and a positive reinforcement of why you have created this business relationship for yourself.

For those unfamiliar with the new home sales process, or for those who would like to know more about how they can benefit − and profit − from selling new homes, this book serves as an introduction to the lucrative opportunities that are available.

Depending on the market conditions where you are, builders may be doing relatively well and making sales at or very close to their published sales price without any promotions or concessions.

In other markets, builders might be willing to work with you and your buyers to achieve a mutually satisfactory sales price.

New home prices in some areas are tempered by short sales and foreclosures, but a never-before-occupied, brand new home will serve your customers well and earn you the maximum commission over a distressed property.

Plus, a builder's warranty is going to apply on new homes as well as all of the manufacturer's warranties for the appliances, fixtures, and systems.

Builders want to sell homes, and they know that you are a valuable resource for producing people who can purchase what they are offering — already constructed or to-be-built.

As you read the following pages, begin to imagine or visualize how this can apply to you and how you can begin making money by working with builders.

This is a very efficient use of your time. Plus, it gives your customers a worry-free home than is backed by the builder for workmanship and merchantability for at least a year.

Even better, the builder takes care of processing the sale so you can pursue additional business.

Selling With Builders

*How Realtors® Can
Profit From Selling
Builders' New Homes*

1

What's In It For You?

Overview Of Residential Sales

Let's begin by looking at how you make money in real estate.

You can be a listing agent who gets paid when a home you list for sale is sold, or you can be a buyer's agent or transactional agent who helps sell property and gets paid when that sale happens.

How much you make depends on the number of other agents involved in the transaction, the amount or percentage of the commission, and the sales price.

The properties that you work with can be either residential or non-residential (commercial). However, our focus in this book is residential real estate.

In residential real estate — not counting land sales or leasing — essentially you are involved in helping private individuals buy and sell existing homes ("resales") or in showing and selling brand new homes, that are offered by builders, to interested and qualified customers.

Your Focus

You may decide to specialize in either resales or new home sales, or you may use a combination of both.

You may decide to concentrate primarily on the listing part of the business by identifying and meeting with people who are interested in marketing and selling their current homes with you.

Possibly your emphasis is or will be on working as a buyer's agent (or representative) and helping people locate and acquire a different residence (either new or existing).

Perhaps a major aspect of your business is or will be working with people relocating to your area, working mainly with investors looking for rental income properties, or focusing on first-time buyers.

You might focus on short sales, foreclosures, and bank owned properties (REO).

There are so many ways to make money in residential real estate today.

Regardless of your present emphasis, however, selling new homes that builders have available as already built homes or as pre-sales for delivery later can be a significant — and potentially quite lucrative — part of your real estate business.

Expanding Into New Home Sales

If you've already shown new homes to your customers by taking them to a builder's model home, sales center, kiosk, or storefront location, that's great.

However, if you've never visited a builder's model center with a customer or been inclined to do so, I encourage you to consider it as a way of expanding your business.

It can be very profitable to work with builders, and as the number of your new home transactions increases, your time management also improves.

This will help you enjoy your business more, give you some time off occasionally, allow you time to run your errands, and let you pursue other aspects of your business like prospecting, attending a seminar, or meeting with new customers.

When you show and sell new homes, the builders and their onsite sales staffs will assist you in producing the sales and in processing the paperwork.

It's a total team effort, and you're the beneficiary.

Therefore, you should consider the positive business ramifications that can accrue to you by expanding your real estate sales career to include the sale of new homes.

Keeping An Open Mind

If you're not that familiar with the new home sales process and what it's all about, that's OK.

That's what I want to acquaint you with so that you understand the financial possibilities available for you.

I want you to understand how builders typically work with Realtors® like you and with potential buyers — regardless of how you are attracted to their location.

Some people will initially learn about or contact a builder (by phone, email, or in-person) through a website or internet listing, blog, or article. They quite likely will use some type of search terms or phrase that will lead them to that builder and other new homes in that area.

Others will rely on signage, ads, and other sources — including Realtors® such as you. So, please keep an open-mind about the advantages of working with builders.

When you choose to make selling builders' homes a part of your overall business strategy, you'll find that this is a great way to make money and save time.

You'll also broaden your options because many people only want to look at builders' models (new homes) or want to visit several of them as part of their decision-making process.

Remaining Independent

As I talk about working with builders — or "partnering" or selling with them — let's be clear about what is meant.

I'm not talking about or implying a formal relationship of any kind. I'm not talking about an employment relationship either.

I'm certainly not talking about you going to work for the builder as an employee or contracting with them to sit their model home for them (although you may wish to do that through your broker).

I'm talking about creating a strategic, transactional, temporary business relationship with builders to produce a sale with your customer. It might happen just once, or it be something you continue to do.

There's nothing that creates a binding relationship or any type of expectation by the builders for you to perform or act in a certain way.

When I talk about selling the builders' homes, it's strictly from the standpoint of you connecting your customers with the various new home choices that are available to them and letting them decide if they want to own a new home that you are showing them.

A sale is made because there is a need and a solution, and you are the procuring cause. That's all.

You remain an independent real estate professional with no ties to any particular builder – only a transactional relationship as a buyer's agent when you introduce your customers to the builder's offerings.

You are not working *for* a builder, you are working *with* a builder. This is a very important distinction.

Creating A New Focus

With the essentially unlimited opportunities to show and sell new homes with builders – relying on their ability to build new homes and thus create new listings on a perpetual and consistent basis, as well as their capacity to process the sale – you have the ability to generate a substantial part of your business by focusing on the new home market.

Therefore, you have a choice in how you want to approach your real estate sales business.

You can choose to earn your living exclusively by listing, selling, and showing existing older homes – traditional resales, short sales, foreclosures, REOs, and other distressed properties – or you can make a conscious decision to increase your income opportunities and your potential to show attractive properties by participating with builders in selling their new homes.

In fact, some Realtors® choose to concentrate solely on showing and selling just new homes.

It All Begins With The Listing

As you know, selling any residential property begins with the listing – regardless of how that listing is created or who does it.

Essentially, a willing seller agrees to part with his or her property for mutually agreeable terms and to compensate the listing agent (you or someone like you) for helping that to occur (either entirely as the listing and selling agent or as a co-broker bringing a buyer to an already existing listing).

To be successful in the resale market, you continually need to add to your funnel by identifying potential buyers and sellers and creating or acting upon additional listings.

You either need to continue to create listings – if you focus on that side of the business – or you need to locate and identify existing listings to share with your potential buyers.

However, contrast this with the dynamics that exist in the new home market that builders create. Homebuilders supply listings that are plentiful and renewable.

When you decide to form a strategic alliance with builders to create a temporary, transactional, "joint-venture" relationship with them, they provide the products ("listings") and you supply the consumers ("buyers").

Depending on the size of your market and the number of builders, there are always listings available – for building lots, home under construction, or completed dwellings at various price points.

Builders Have Ready-Made Listings

Because the builders are making their properties available for sale to the public – sometimes on the MLS and sometimes not – these are listings that you can have access to just by being aware of them.

You can show and sell these listings to your customers through your temporary relationship with any builder.

Builders across your marketplace have several listings (posted or not) of brand new, never-before-occupied new homes from which to choose for your customers.

Not all of them are completed homes. Some are already built and are ready for immediate occupancy or quick delivery as soon as the processing is completed. Others are sold on a to-be-built basis.

Some are even in a "near completion" stage where the home is ready to be completed within 30-60 days but with interior final touches remaining to be done and selected by your customers.

This means that your buyers could still choose the style, color, and finish of such items as carpeting, wall paint, cabinets, countertops, floor and wall tile, and other items to personalize their new home. They just don't have to wait as long for their new home to be completed as they would if they were starting the entire construction process from scratch.

No Need To Reinvent Anything

Regardless of what stage of completion the new homes are in — from completed homes to vacant homesites or somewhere in between — these listings that builders are offering are ones that you do not need to create but merely act upon.

You can just use your time to focus on making sales and satisfying your customers — with a new home product.

The homes — decorated models, homes under construction, and those already completed — are there for you anytime you want to show them. The vacant homesites are as well.

Furthermore, these listings are for never-before-occupied new homes — typically with a performance warranty for several years as well.

There also is a great potential for even more new homes through additional listings — when a particular builder that you enjoy working with sells all of his or her new homes ("current listings") in one location and then offers homes ("new listings") in other locations for you to help sell.

Some builders are willing to build on your customer's site as well – and will compensate you for producing the sale just the same as if they were building the home on a vacant homesite they already owned.

Built-In Time Savings

One of the great things about using builder's listings to show to your customers is the huge amount of time that you'll save by having the ready-made listings.

If you normally take listings as part of your business, you know how much time it takes to prepare for a presentation, complete your market research, do a CMA, and meet with your potential sellers to attempt to secure the listing agreement.

Then, if there are questions that you need to research, or you have to return for a second appointment, there's the additional time for that.

When you sell new homes with a builder, the homesites and homes are already "listed."

There's no need to do anything in advance except have a general idea of what the builder offers in terms of size and price range and determine if that meets the requirements of your buyers. Then you just show up with your customers.

There's no need for CMAs or evening appointments to make a presentation and secure a listing. The listings are there for you to show – generally all in one place.

Treat them as you would any other listings. The builder is essentially the listing broker, and you are the selling side.

You'll just be eliminating a lot of time that normally would be spent to generate the listings and to locate various properties to look at scattered about your market area.

Builders Want Your Help

Builders are interested in selling their homes and in creating satisfied customers. That's why they are in business. That's also how they make money and stay in business.

That's where you come into the picture.

Builders have several ways to generate leads and potential purchasers for their new homes, including advertising.

However, they know that you are a valuable resource capable of producing qualified people who want to purchase what they are offering.

They recognize that you have a great exposure to the marketplace and that you have access to people looking for homes that they don't.

They know that people rely on your opinions for helping them to select their next home.

Therefore, they want your help and will compensate you for your ability to produce a bona fide customer that can conclude a transaction. They welcome and actively invite your participation with them.

No Experience Necessary

When you walk into a builder's model home or sales center, it doesn't matter if you are there for the first time or if you've been there previously.

It also doesn't matter if you are showing up with a potential buyer or if you are going in advance to learn about what is available.

Actually, you might feel more comfortable in selecting which builders to focus on and "partner" with if you arrange to visit them by yourself or with others from your office to "preview" what is available and become acquainted with their operation — before taking a customer with you. This will let you experience the properties for yourself at a relaxed pace.

If there wasn't time for that preview visit because you had a willing buyer who wanted to see what a particular builder offered, then you and your customers will have learned about the builder together — and formed your opinions about the quality of their operation and what they offered.

Giving It A Chance

The goal in all of this is for you to make sales, for the builders to make sales, and for your customers to get a home they want at a great value.

As you keep reading, you'll discover even more reasons why working with a builder should make sense for you and your customers.

Selling new homes with a builder is a great way for your customers to get a brand new home and for you to make money — and to allow you to use your time more efficiently than typical with resales.

2

Additional Benefits For You

A Builder Is Not A Typical Seller

A builder is different from any other seller that you might encounter.

A builder is not the typical owner of a home who wants to sell it in order to buy another one that more closely meets their needs than what they have now.

A person listing and selling their own property with you or another agent has just that one property involved.

A builder, on the other hand, may have dozens of properties available at the same time — possibly in various sizes, styles, price ranges, and maybe even in different locations in your area.

Some of the homes may already be built and completed, some may be in partial stages of completion, and others may be just floor plans for vacant homesites.

In addition, builders are going to take an active role in marketing and selling their listings — unlike the typical homeowner with a house to sell. Also, they are not emotionally attached to their homes.

Builders Sell Their Own Properties

While you have several different properties that you can show to someone — from the hundreds of properties that are in the MLS or from pocket listings that you or your office might have — builders only have their own properties to show you.

Since builders — directly or through their onsite sales representatives — have just their own properties to sell, they work at becoming experts on those properties.

They can take the time to become specialists on what they build.

They are familiar with all of the characteristics and features of their homes so they can help you and your customers evaluate them effectively.

They also know the potential homesites or locations that are available — and the particular features and benefits of each.

In some cases, builders will build on scattered sites they have, on the customer's lot, or in other communities where they have been building, but normally when you visit a builder's office, you are just going to hear about and see the homes that you came to see — in the neighborhood that you came to look at and nowhere else.

Builders do not have a hidden agenda. Their purpose is quite clear. They want to sell *their* new homes.

Letting Builders Work For You

You may have a good first-hand experience of what builders are offering in your area and feel that you could show your customers what is available at various new home communities or builders' model homes.

However, your ability to show the model homes to your customers is not the issue.

When you take customers to see a builder's model, learn to rely on the builder or their onsite sales staffs to show their homes and help you make a sale to your customers.

It's their fulltime responsibility to know everything about their own listings and to show them to you and your customers in such a way that they convey everything that is important for your customers to be able to make an informed decision.

Going With The Flow

Even if you could show the model to your customers by yourself because you have seen that home many times, respect the business relationship that is being created between you and the builder and allow them to show you and your customers the model — or other floor plans that might be available — and talk about their company and how they do business.

It's their show while you are with them so let them earn their listing commission by helping you to make the sale. This takes a lot of the pressure away from you to make the sale and puts it squarely on them.

Besides, there may have been something changed, added, or upgraded since your last visit. Maybe financing, incentives, availability, or some of the features might be different since your last visit or contact.

You may like to go on your own with your customers to look at the home and not have the builders or their representatives accompany you, but let them take you through the home and acquaint you with what is in it. Then they'll give you time to be alone to experience the home and talk among yourselves. If they don't offer, request it.

Builders Respect Your Relationship

Builders regard you as a very important and influential source of potential sales. Also, they cherish your goodwill and positive word-of-mouth advertising.

They respect your relationship with any customers that you might produce, and they would not do anything intentionally to damage their business relationship with you or your company.

They know that your customers accompanied you to their model center and that they will leave with you.

Builders know that you can help them make sales by "lending" them (not relinquishing or turning over) your customers that you have generated so that a successful transaction might occur.

In turn, they rely on you to assist them — both by encouraging your customers to make a decision on a new home and in reinforcing the positive aspects of what they have available for your customers.

Cooperation (and trust) between you and the builder — as well as his or her onsite sales staff — is essential for a sustained, successful working relationship.

Builders Are Not Competition

Builders are in the new home business — not resales. They are not in competition with you for listings of resales or in trying to make sales to your customers other than what is available through their new homes.

They are there to serve you and your customers — as well as other customers that they generate on their own through their other forms of marketing.

In fact, most builders do not even operate a general realty office in addition to or in conjunction with their new home operation.

They make their income from selling land to consumers (which they already have acquired or control) or from building and delivering a new home to go along with the land.

They would prefer to sell a new home directly to the consumer, but if the only way to meet the customer's needs is to offer an existing home (usually one that they built and sold previously), some builders want to have that flexibility through a resale function of homes in their community — or through participation with a Realtor® like you to list those homes for them.

Sometimes they function as the broker and list their own properties in their community. Other times they list those homes with someone like you so be aware of these possibilities also.

The primary goal of builders is to sell a *new* home — not a resale.

They definitely do not want to compete with you in the resale market.

General Realty Activities Are Rare

When builders do have a general realty function, their listings rarely include any homes that they didn't build originally or ones they need to sell for a customer to facilitate a new home purchase.

Typically, there is a separate realty operation with different personnel or locations for those functions.

Again, the instances of this are rare.

Nevertheless, here is another opportunity for you to work with builders to help them move those resale homes in their communities.

Builders Are Location Specific

When builders have an onsite sales staff, those salespeople only are paid for selling a new home at their own location — the one where you are visiting with them.

In fact, they rarely discuss homes available at other company locations.

Most of them do not receive any compensation (such as a referral fee, finder's fee or commission split) for sending or taking a customer to a "sister community" when they are unable to meet a particular customer's needs at their own location. Thus, they are motivated to show you something that will work for your customers at their location.

This is another reason why they don't leave their site, why they won't take you and your customers offsite to any other location, and why they're very good at knowing their own product.

Therefore, trust them to do everything in their power to make a sale with you at their location.

Do not worry about them attempting to make a sale at any other location or to discuss a resale property. It just isn't how they work.

Builders Handle The Paperwork

A great aspect of selling homes with a builder is that all of the paperwork is handled for you.

All of the necessary day-to-day activities that are required to complete and process the sale are completed by the builders or their staffs — freeing you to pursue other parts of your business or just have a little personal time.

This means that while the builders are processing your sale, you can secure new listings, conduct showings of listed properties, host open houses, meet new potential customers, and produce sales of other properties. You can even get in an afternoon of fun on the golf course or at the beach if you like.

Compared to a resale transaction where you or your office would need to coordinate or complete the necessary documents, inspections, and other activities that lead to closing of the sale, the builders or their staffs make sure that these actions are completed or coordinated.

This includes completing all of the paperwork (including any applicable addenda, approvals, verifications, contingencies, inspections, notifications, or disclosures).

It also means preparing an estimate of closing costs, maintaining and accounting for escrow monies (and depositing them), expediting the mortgage approval process (when applicable), initiating or facilitating the mortgage application and all of the forms that are required to be submitted by the buyer, monitoring the approval and processing of the application (even when the customer's lender is used), and getting the sale ready for closing.

This is a tremendous advantage and timesavings for you.

Builders Help Your Customers

In addition to doing and processing all of the paperwork and forms necessary to conclude the sale and get the new home ready for your customers to move into it, the builders or their teams help your customers personalize their new home selection to make it just right for them.

This includes the customary choices as well as special ones that put their mark on their new home.

Since most buyers will want to personalize or customize their new home, the builders (or their onsite representatives or selections coordinators) will assist your customers with the selection of colors and finishes on the exterior siding (or brick or stucco), shutters, trim, doors, and roofing as well as applicable included features (such as flooring, appliances, bathroom fixtures, trim colors, interior doors, lighting fixtures, cabinet and door hardware, countertops and cabinets) and the choice of any additional or custom features, including special order items.

During the construction, the builders or their personnel will arrange for your purchasers to have access to their new home (along with you if you want to accompany them) for periodic inspections of the progress.

Throughout the process, the builders and their teams are available to answer questions and communicate information to you and your customers to keep everyone informed of what is happening. You and your customers should be updated regularly.

Builders Get The Closing Ready

Prior to closing of the sale and transfer of title to your customers, the builders or their teams make sure that all of the required forms and procedures are completed, such as termite certification, surveys, appraisals, title insurance policies, certificate of occupancy or final inspection, title search or abstract, and homeowner's warranty.

Then they will coordinate with the title company or the closing agent for the closing of title and disbursement of funds (including your commission).

You are welcome to accompany your customers to the closing table, but it's not a requirement. The builder's title company will handle everything if you choose not to be present.

Builders Want To Keep You Informed

The builders want you and your customers to be aware of exactly how the sale is progressing toward the move-in date and closing, so they will keep you and your purchasers informed about the status of items in process.

The more you and your customers know about what is going on and how everything is moving along, the more satisfied you are going to be with the process.

While the home is being completed or made ready, they will advise you of various details, such as when the appraisal was ordered, when it was completed, any additional deposits that are due, verification of employment and banking information, mortgage loan processing status, mortgage loan approval date, last date to make any changes, and completion and delivery status on the home.

Once the home is ready to close, the builder's office will notify you and your customers about the scheduled walk-through/pre-closing inspection and orientation date, and the scheduled closing date.

Helping Your Customers Adjust

Prior to move-in, the builders or their representatives will help orient your customers to their new neighborhood and the community association (if there is one), introduce them to existing residents, show them through the community, and discuss key services and facilities in the surrounding area.

They will help your customers transfer their mail service, arrange for utility service (electric, gas, and water), and establish telephone, internet, and cable or satellite TV connections.

Then the staff members will monitor the satisfaction of your customers with their new homes after occupancy, take care of post-occupancy maintenance and repair issues, make sure that your customers know how to operate all of the fixtures and equipment in their new home, show them how to contact the appropriate staff person for any type of post-delivery service, administer the warranty program, and be available to answer questions about their new home, the neighborhood, and services in the area.

Builders Are There For You

Builders make working with them convenient and efficient.

They maintain a model center where you can show your customers new homes and they can select the one that is right for them. They explain to you and your customers what is available so that an informed decision can be made.

They process all of the paperwork and the details to get the sale closed and funded.

They orient your customers to their new homes so that the buying experience and transition into their new home will be pleasant and as seamless as possible.

They keep you informed so that you will understand that they truly appreciate your business and that they are there to serve you.

3

New Homes Versus Resales

New Home And Resales Are Different

While some resale opportunities rival new homes for their location and included features, they differ in that they aren't brand new and they can't be personalized or customized prior to delivery.

Since many resales have been built quite recently, they may have many appliances, fixtures, and technologies that new homes offer — but there can be major differences in the condition of the homes and the paperwork involved to process the sale.

When you sell a new home by working temporarily with a builder to make that happen, your customers are assured of getting a brand new home, and all of the inspections, notifications, and paperwork required to get the sale to the closing table are handled by the builders.

Selling A New Home Versus A Resale

The whole process of selling a new home is different from that involved in working with a resale.

First, the builders and their teams take care of accomplishing many of the details associated with processing the sale of a new home and getting it ready to close — so your purchasers can move in and you can be paid.

Working with builders to sell a new home requires much less effort than showing and selling a resale. This saves you a tremendous amount of time that you can use as you like — including pouring it right back into your business in other areas.

Contrast the sale of a new home where the builders help you present the property and process the sale with what typically is required when you sell a resale or existing home.

With a new home, many of the typical, required, or customary activities that are required to conclude a transaction with a resale and get it ready for occupancy simply are not necessary.

It's Already Listed

For starters, you won't need to identify and meet with a potential seller and obtain or renew a listing agreement. The listing already exists.

You also won't need to present any offers or counteroffers to either party.

Additionally, you won't need do any CMAs prior to the listing appointment or prepare, file, and maintain MLS data.

There's no need to be concerned about the condition of the home that the previous owners or occupants have left it in, any unusual paint schemes or decorations, any odors or stains, any undisclosed material defects, or repairs that might be pending or necessary.

Your customers can still get a home inspection done for themselves — and many new home purchasers choose to do this — but it really isn't necessary except to indicate some punchlist items.

All appliances, fixtures, and systems should be working fine, but you and your customers can determine this to your satisfaction at the pre-closing inspection.

Any items requiring attention will be addressed immediately while your customers are present, before closing, or within the first 30-days after occupancy.

Resales Require More Work

When you sell new homes with a builder, you won't need to erect and maintain yard signs, inspect and create an inventory of the seller's appliances or fixtures, determine which items are personal property, and find out the age and condition of the major appliances, heating and cooling systems, roof, and other major components of the home.

You won't need to determine which conditions exist that materially affect the value of the property that need to be documented, disclosed, and also possibly rectified or repaired by the seller. You won't need to document any repairs that have been completed or ones that are necessary.

Other *unnecessary* activities in working with a new home compared to a resale include preparing and running newspaper ads, updating your website and MLS information, managing and accounting for marketing or advertising budgets, driving by and checking on the condition of your listings, arranging for and scheduling appointments to show listings, installing lock boxes or maintaining codes or keys, arranging for and hosting open houses, scheduling inspections and having them conducted, dealing with the seller's personal property or pets and the physical appearance of the property during showings or open houses, and answering telephone or email inquiries — from both the public and other agents or brokers.

No Money To Handle

When you work with a resale home and get an offer on it, there's always money to receive, handle, deposit, and account for.

If you are the selling agent, you have to get a deposit (binder, earnest money, good faith money) check or cash from your customers that you can show or present to the sellers or their agent along with the offer to purchase.

You have to safeguard this money until the seller or their agent accepts the money and gives you a receipt for it.

If you are the selling agent, you have to receipt the deposit that you receive and deposit it in your escrow account or deliver it to your broker for deposit.

When you sell a new home, the builders handle all of the money. Your customers tender an initial deposit —

cash, check, or credit card — from a few dollars to the entire initial deposit required directly to the builders, and you never have to touch it.

Model Homes Are Kept Ready To Show

A very big difference between showing and selling a builder's model home and a resale property is the interior condition of each — and how your customers are received at each.

A new home model center is a retail location that maintains regular posted office hours. As long as you arrive during those normal business hours, you can expect it to be open and ready for business.

It is staffed during those hours to answer questions for you and help you and your customers evaluate the opportunities available — and to select a new home that meets their needs.

It is designed to represent the best of what a builder can deliver and often is decorated and furnished in the latest colors and styles.

It may contain a number of graphics, displays, and other signage to explain, inform, and illustrate what is available. These are for reference points as well as for education.

Just Drop In

You may choose to call ahead to a builder to let them know you're coming with a customer so they can be prepared to spend some time with you and your customers, but you never have to call ahead to make sure the house is picked up, or that it's clean, or that no one is home from school or work with the flu or a cold.

You don't have to use a lockbox to gain entry. The door is unlocked. Just open it and walk in.

You don't have to worry about walking into a vacant home that has a closed-up smell or an occupied home with unpleasant odors.

There should be no concerns about the temperature being wrong for the season (too hot and stuffy in the summer or too chilly in the winter) or not being able to turn on enough lights or turn off the security alarm.

No Pets Or Children

In a model home, unlike a home that someone is living in, you never need to worry about catching someone in their bathrobe or pajamas if you just drop in. The model home is open and just sitting there ready for you to arrive and begin your tour.

You don't have to wait until it's convenient for the sellers before you arrive. You're not waiting for them to pick up the living room or clear the table of dishes.

You don't need to worry about making sure the pets are put away or that your customers might have pet allergies that would make them uncomfortable looking at the home — or that there might be lingering animal smells that detract from showing and experiencing the home.

You don't need to be concerned about homework spread out on the kitchen table, or a partially painted wall that hasn't been completed, or the lawn which didn't get cut, or the leftover aroma of lasagna from the night before, or burnt toast from breakfast — or anything else that might make the home look lived in and comfortable but does not lend itself to viewing it objectively.

That also means not having to be concerned about toys that haven't been put away, beds unmade, or clothes that haven't been picked up.

New Homes Come With Warranties

Aside from the many other benefits (including a significant amount of time savings) that accrue to you (and your customers) when you show and sell a new home with a builder, new homes come with several warranties to provide you and your buyers with peace-of-mind.

As I mentioned, home inspections to check on systems and possible hidden defects are unnecessary with a new home.

You can order them and pay for them, but they really aren't beneficial except for identifying a punchlist item that you possibly overlooked.

By law in most states, the builder is liable and responsible for taking care of any issues that arise during the initial year of occupancy on a new home.

Beyond that, builders may have additional warranties that they offer. They may even provide an insured third-party warranty program that provides as much as a 10-year program of total protection for major structural components and workmanship.

Also, the major components and fixtures, such as appliances, roofing materials, windows, siding, heating and cooling systems, water heaters, bath fixtures, flooring, cabinets, siding, electrical systems, and similar items are new and warrantied by their manufacturer or supplier for specific periods of time and terms.

New Homes Are Built To Code

Additionally, new homes are designed and built to the latest building and zoning codes and specifications.

This includes requirements for materials used in the construction of the homes that are tested to withstand major regional weather phenomena, such as snow, ice, hail, earthquakes, or hurricanes.

The homes are required to be built at a sufficient elevation above the crown of the road to be able to protect the homes from standing water that would result from heavy rainfall.

There is even a flood insurance program available for homes located in a flood prone area, such as a low-lying area or near a river.

In addition, builders are certified contractors and they use other certified and licensed subcontractors and tradespeople in the construction of their new homes.

The home designs and site plans have been or will be (in the case of a to-be-built home) reviewed for adherence to the latest codes prior to the issuance of a building permit and then inspected regularly throughout the construction process to make sure they continue to comply with these requirements.

With a new home, there is no concern over lead paint that might have been used at sometime in the past or the presence of asbestos in insulation, flooring, or ceiling materials.

Other outmoded or prohibited building products will not be a concern either.

This cuts down on the notifications required to be furnished to your customers and gives you and them additional peace of mind.

Builders Want Your Participation

Builders have a product for which they need customers (that you can supply), and they essentially are able to provide that product (or a similar one in a different location) on a continuous basis.

Meanwhile, you have access to qualified, potential customers for their product.

They recognize that you are capable of supplying consumers for them on a consistent basis, and they are willing to pay you for producing a purchaser.

Then they will complete and manage the day-to-day details associated with the transaction, allowing you to concentrate on working with other customers and making sales with those customers — and they are offering a product that competes extremely favorably against resales. In fact, in many areas, new homes are beyond comparison.

Selling new homes with builders and their representatives is a great way to expand your real estate business and increase your income — and it's a great way to manage your time more efficiently as well.

4

Getting Started

Identifying Builders That You Trust

Since you are creating a temporary, informal, strategic, transactional alliance with a particular homebuilder each time you show his or her new homes or homesites to a prospective purchaser — and ultimately generate a sales transaction — you need to be comfortable with the various relationships you establish.

You don't need to work with every builder — or any specific builders. It's a business decision. I think the merits of working with builders are strong, but it's your choice about who you want to "partner" with.

There's no pressure to work with any certain builders or any particular number of them — if any. Part of your decision is going to be made by what types of homes your customers might be interested in looking at and owning, and part is going to be made by who you like working with.

You need to take time to do your homework and make sure that the builders you select are worthy of your trust and affiliation.

Doing Your Homework

You'll get paid for producing a sale with most any builder for which you produce a willing buyer, but you want to make sure you enjoy the sales process.

Therefore, you should seek out and work with just those builders that you like and respect.

First, identify which builders or new home communities are in your personal market area, or locate ones who offer homes that might appeal to your customers — in terms of size, price, amenities, location, lifestyle, design, quality, appearance, value, and similar factors.

Then, just as you would with any resale property that you might be interested in showing to a prospective purchaser, you need to familiarize yourself in advance with any new home properties that you intend to show and learn about their important features and selling points.

Satisfy yourself about the quality and value of what is being offered, and make sure that you can attach your name to the potential transaction.

Remember you are looking into establishing a possible business relationship as you consider each builder in your area.

You don't need to work with every builder — only those builders that you feel comfortable with and trust.

Learning Firsthand About The Builders

Make time in your schedule to visit personally with any builder or the builder's onsite representative that you are considering working with before you ever take a customer there.

Allow enough time to make a fair assessment of how well you like that builder and what they build.

This way, you can determine — at a relaxed pace — if this is a builder that you want to work with, and you can ask questions freely without being concerned about impacting a particular customer's experience.

Use this opportunity to learn all you can about each builder that you might consider working with.

Become comfortable recommending this builder to your customers and working with him or her to help your customers achieve their goals.

Determining What's Going On

As you meet with each builder or their representative, learn who they are, their building philosophy, their history, the relative degree of satisfaction people have in working with them, their financial stability, their staying power, and their reputation.

Determine what they build — the product type and design, number and mix of homes, how title is conveyed to the purchasers, number of homes planned, number already completed, those under construction or permitted, and how much longer they think it will take to build out that location.

Learn about their construction style, how they approach building their homes, and the quality of materials and workmanship used.

Find out about the availability of furnished models, which floor plans are represented, other floor plans that are offered but not represented by models, included features, customization or modifications allowed, and popular optional features that are available or commonly requested.

Also, look at available homesites (and their characteristics), building requirements, construction schedules, inventory homes available for immediate or relatively quick occupancy, customer support and warranty programs, special incentives, neighborhood services, procedure for purchase, and financing.

Learn about the community recreational amenities, lifestyle opportunities, owner's association, services provided (such as security), and rules and regulations.

Find out about the monthly fees your customers would be responsible for if they lived there and how those monies are allocated for services.

Asking Your Questions

Discover all you can about the builder and his or her sales staff to know what you can expect later when you arrive with a valued customer — and to avoid any surprises concerning or impacting your relationship with that builder.

This is the time to ask about anything that you want to know — anything that will help you feel comfortable in working with a particular builder and then, in turn, recommending this builder to your customers and taking them to see the opportunities available from that builder.

Get your questions answered. Nothing is too minor, insignificant, or silly if it helps you make a decision about working with this builder.

Find out about the builder, the construction process, the new home community, the new home sales process, or anything else about what and how they build their homes.

In some cases, it might be a larger planned community with a central sales pavilion where the sales team represents more than one builder.

If that's the case, you'll want to learn what to expect from the various builders and determine if you are comfortable working with all of the builders in that community or just certain ones.

Stating Your Concerns

During your "preview" visit, raise any objections or concerns that are important to you — or ones that you think your potential customers might have.

Decide if this is a builder that you would like to participate with to show and sell new homes.

Get your concerns answered to your satisfaction — even if you have to meet with more than one person or have someone call you back later with the answer or explanation.

This is the perfect time to explore any and all concerns that you have. There is no immediate sale riding on the outcome of your questions and objections – or their responses.

Without your customers being present, you have the freedom and flexibility to ask why something was done or not done a certain way, why various features or brands were included or excluded, and what changes can be made or considered by a prospective purchaser.

Don't hold back. Satisfy yourself that this is a competent builder that you can wholeheartedly endorse to your customers.

Finding Out How To Make A Sale

As you are evaluating and determining if a builder is one that you want to work with, find out how you would participate in making a sale with them and what generally happens when you arrive there with a customer.

Find out how the actual sales transaction occurs and how it is processed.

Make sure you find out how to register a customer.

Determine if you must be present when you bring a new customer to visit their sales center, or if phone, fax, text, or email registrations are allowed.

Do you have to be present on each subsequent visit?

What if your customers — after the initial visit — just return to the model center on their own or without letting you know ahead of time?

What is the protection period and can it be renewed or extended? For what period of time?

What is the amount of compensation, and how and when you are to be paid?

Learn what specific language in the purchase agreement means or why it is included.

Go ahead and get a brochure and copies of the forms used to register a customer so that you can read over them and be ready when you return with your first customer.

Ask to look at the paperwork that is used to get the sale started — including the purchase agreement, the addenda, and the community bylaws.

Feeding Your Curiosity

This is the time to ask about anything that you are curious about — whether material, important, or just something that catches your interest.

Find out the status of something that is under construction or is in progress, learn if your customer can make changes, ask about pricing changes that might be contemplated or planned, determine additional improvements that are scheduled or planned, and learn about the phasing of construction.

Discover how you and your customers will be kept informed of what is happening at their community — newsletters, texts, emails, faxes, flyers, letters, web updates, social media posts, or telephone calls.

Determine to your satisfaction how you'll be kept up to date about progress toward a sale or closing with any of your customers that you might take there — phone calls, emails, faxes, text messages, and copies of correspondence.

Mainly, be very comfortable with the potential working relationship that you are attempting to create. Only work with those builders whom you like, respect, and trust to work with you and your customers fairly.

Scheduling A "Preview" Appointment

While you can just drop in to see the model or meet with the builder or his or her onsite representative, it's best to call and schedule a specific time for your "preview" visit. Call to make an appointment.

This way, the builders or their representatives can set aside the time necessary to give you a comprehensive understanding of what they are building.

You'll have a chance to see the furnished model (or models) and inspect them.

You'll get to tour the neighborhood or community at a relaxed pace — including any recreational amenities or special features.

You can ask your questions — *without* being concerned about the builders or the representatives being pulled away to work with someone else and without being concerned about impacting the experience of your customers since you will be there by yourself.

Respecting Your Relationship

After you find a builder that you want to work with, make sure that you respect that relationship and honor it.

Do this for each builder that you identify and select.

To get the most out of your business relationship with the builders that you have chosen, ask for them or their representatives on each visit and work just with that specific person you have met.

If there is more than one person staffing the model or sales center — and to accommodate days off and vacations — find out what contingencies or arrangements exist for working with someone else when "your" builders or representatives are not present or are unavailable to work with you and your customers.

It's not a requirement, but it's a good idea to call ahead to arrange a convenient time to arrive with your customers.

This way if there is a conflict or an issue working with the person with whom you have created the relationship, you can arrange a mutually convenient time to visit later that day or whatever works for everyone involved.

Please call to cancel or reschedule an appointment when plans change (for either you or your customers). It's also a good idea to call from your car if you are running more than a few minutes late.

Feeling Comfortable

Do your homework and identify the builders that you want to work with.

Then you can enthusiastically recommend them and present their opportunities to your customers.

From your research and your "preview" visits, you'll know that both you and your customers will be treated professionally and fairly and that your customers will enjoy their experience.

You also know that you'll be protected and paid for your efforts in producing a purchaser.

This is the type of comfort level that will produce a great strategic relationship.

5

Market Factors

Existing Homes Can Be Attractive

As we are talking about showing and selling new homes that builders offer, let's pause for a moment and look at "existing" or "resale" homes in the market.

Your customers may find them attractive — particularly since many of them are relatively new anyway.

With the number of foreclosure, bank-owned, and short sale properties that are a part of many markets, these may present good opportunities for your customers — approaching it from a purchase price basis.

Obviously, to get a well-built home, in a good neighborhood, with many of the latest features or design trends, it's not always necessary to buy a brand new home.

Recently Built Home Compare Well

Many existing homes are available in established neighborhoods that are desirable for their location or character, and some existing homes in older neighborhoods have been remodeled or refurbished to include modern, up-to-date interior features.

Also, many existing homes that are on the market have been built within the past few years.

Thus, people can find relatively new homes that are located in neighborhoods similar to where new homes are available.

Many people may feel that they can get a relatively new home that in many ways has the latest features and styling as a new home and perhaps save some money over buying a new home — and this largely is true.

Keep in mind that we are not talking about any inventory of already built new homes that a builder might have but the resales of homes that have been occupied or at least owned by someone other than the builder.

Two Distinct Advantages Of New Homes

A recently built home in a new community or a well-maintained home in an established neighborhood may have appeal for some of your buyers and offer many of the same advantages as getting a new home.

However, some people just desire a new home.

Additionally, there are two special advantages that a new home offers over a resale or just a newer or different home.

The first is financial, and the second is just the fact that it is something new.

The Financial Advantage

Some people are only interested in purchasing a new home or lean in that direction for the financial advantage.

They feel that their investment will be protected better, that the chances of appreciation are greater, that the builder is standing behind the quality and workmanship through a warranty program as well as their reputation, that energy costs are going to be lower, or that the financing programs are better with a new home.

For people who have never owned a home before, they feel that they would do better to invest in something new since they are not experienced homeowners.

They don't want to be concerned with maintenance issues. They know that that the appliances and other major components are new and that they come with warranties.

They know that the builder takes care of many of the little cosmetic issues in the home as well.

Knowing that items aren't likely to break or need repaired immediately — and the fact that if they do the builder will take care of them — is a major financial consideration for selecting a new home over a resale.

The "Something New" Advantage

In addition to the financial advantage that owning a new home has over a resale, some people just like the idea of just owning something new. Obviously, a resale can't satisfy this objective — no matter what else it has going for it or how much it would like to.

There are many recently built existing homes that compare favorably with new homes in terms of the features they offer, and several newly established neighborhoods have comparable amenities to brand new communities. Still, nothing can say "new" like a new home.

People want a home that no one else has occupied previously — that also includes the latest, most up-to-date features and technology.

They also want to be the ones to select the colors and styles of the interior finishes and features — and the first ones to spill that glass of grape juice, red wine, or Kool-Aid on the new carpet.

Plus, they want to personalize their new home with special additional features.

With a new home, there is no concern over hidden defects, the presence of banned substances or building materials, or how the home may have been cared for. There are no worries about inheriting someone else's maintenance issues.

Moving Into A Resale

Even when a new home hasn't been selected and someone buys a resale home, the first thing that happens as they prepare to move in is that they personalize their new home.

They want to put their own stamp on it — to brand it as their own.

They want to remove as many traces of the previous owners as they can so they immediately go to work cleaning and disinfecting their new home throughout, they repaint the walls, and they replace all of the carpeting.

They may switch out some of the cabinet hardware, faucets, shower curtains, light switches, and other easily changed items also.

Many people even factor this additional expense and time into their offering price.

Buying a new home with a builder eliminates these issues. They aren't a factor.

No one has lived in the home prior to delivery so disinfecting it, changing out items, or painting walls isn't necessary. Also, the builder cleans each home before the closing.

Financial Concerns Of Buying A Home

As you know, owning a home is a major emotional as well as financial commitment. It is typically the largest single investment that people make.

Your customers may be concerned about honoring and meeting this substantial financial obligation, and that might be holding them back a little on making a decision.

They may have concerns about layoffs, work stoppages, the future of their company, disabilities, health issues, or other things that could interrupt their primary source of income.

Additionally, many people are uncomfortable sharing their financial records and personal information with a lender or other third party and are worried about being rejected for a loan or not qualifying for the terms they had anticipated.

Some people have never owned a home before (new or resale) and making a decision about spending a substantial amount of money is a major step for them.

Concerns About Working With A Builder

Some people are concerned about doing business with a builder because of what they have heard or read.

This is why you need to assure yourself that the builders you have chosen to work with are reputable — then you can convey this comfort level and confidence to your customers.

Let them know that you share and appreciate their concerns and that you have done your homework to be able to satisfy your questions and gain a degree of comfort about working with any builders that you decide to take them to see.

Concerns About Actually Moving

When people are considering a move, they wonder about several issues, such as making new friends for themselves and their family — and locating new services, commuting routes, area activities, and other conveniences.

Change is disruptive and even frightening to some people.

So, as much as people want to move into a new home or find the prospects of doing so an attractive alternative to their current home, the idea of uprooting and moving everything they own into a new home — sometimes miles away from their current location — can be very challenging and quite daunting for some people.

Your reassurance about the process of looking for, locating, and selecting a new home or resale that will meet their needs better than their current home — and moving into it — will help them to accept making a decision and moving forward. Don't underestimate the importance of your role here.

Getting To The Buying Decision Itself

You have helped your customers evaluate all of the reasons that they have for wanting to purchase and occupy a new home (or even a newer or different one than they have currently).

You have helped them factor in the financial reasons and other concerns that they have for not moving from their current home and just remaining where they are.

You have helped them make sense of the various properties that you have shown them that you feel would satisfy their needs.

Now, one thing remains.

If your customers truly desire and want a new, newer, or different home — and they are committed to getting one after they locate the one that will satisfy their needs, wants, budget, and timing — then the only thing standing in the way of that happening is the actual decision to buy it.

This can be a big step for some people.

Some of your customers have never bought a new home before or worked with a builder to get a brand new home. For others, it may have been several years since they have purchased a home.

You may have to help your customers feel comfortable with the idea of making a purchasing decision.

Even though emotionally they are ready to move forward with the home you have helped them select, their fears and apprehensions may be giving them second thoughts about going ahead.

Often a response to fear is to revert to their present home and decide that what they have now is safer, easier, or less stressful than moving.

Supporting The Buying Decision

As you know, some people reach decisions very quickly while others require dozens of facts and take a much longer time to make a decision.

Some will need to visit and re-visit a property many times while other people are ready to make a decision on the initial visit or view.

Some people even try to second-guess themselves or want to change their minds after they make a decision

— or they will delay making a decision until they're "absolutely sure."

Therefore, in addition to being a trusted advisor in helping your customers identify and select a home (a new home or a resale) you also have a cheerleader function to help them feel comfortable that they made the right decision.

When they purchase a new home from a builder, you need to use your insight from getting to know the builder and his or her staff during your preview visits to reassure your customers that the builder will do everything that was promised.

As I have been suggesting, there are many reasons and advantages for your customers to select a brand new home from a builder — whether it is to-be-built, partially completed, or ready for immediate occupancy.

You should help them to feel comfortable with their decision.

Negotiating With Builders

For the longest time, builders would not negotiate on the price of their homes. Everyone paid the published price.

Sometimes there was room for negotiation on the move-in date, financing terms, or additional features — but never on price.

While "submitting an offer" is how a resale home is purchased, this simply wasn't discussed or done in working with builders.

That has largely changed.

Depending on your local market conditions, many builders are now open to making or considering concessions on the price or features included in the home that your buyers want to purchase.

This has come about due to an oversupply of new home inventory (in the market and possibly with that particular builder), short sales and foreclosures that are competing with builders, a general slowdown in real estate sales and the demand for new homes, appraisal issues, the availability of comps, or other economic factors.

Some builders will entertain below-list-price-offers if they seem reasonable or if the terms can be flexible, yet other builders (particularly the smaller ones) will take a more traditional approach to pricing and selling their homes at or near the full published sales price. Doing your homework ahead of time will help.

Builders Have Certain Fixed Costs

Nevertheless, builders have certain fixed costs that factor into the price of their homes — regardless of what the ultimate sales price happens to be or how much they would like the sales price to be.

These include the price of the land, the site improvements, the price of building materials and labor, the cost of construction financing, and required fees and regulatory expenses.

Builders Use Realistic Pricing

In addition to the fixed or hard costs associated with building homes, the builders also have to maintain the model home and sales center and incur expenses such as advertising, marketing, maintenance, and overhead.

Also, the builder has his or her profit, and like any business would like to get a good return on their investment.

In most cases, however, builders operate on a very small profit margin. When they are asked — or when they agree — to take less than the published sales price for a home or to "toss in" a washer, dryer or something else, this reduction comes *directly* from their profit.

Thus, builders attempt to price their homes realistically for ready purchase by prospective homeowners.

They cannot wait for someone to come along to pay inflated prices or a price they'd "like to get" so that they can realize more of a profit.

As long as your customers feel that they are getting good value for their money — regardless of what they pay — and the builder is willing to accept what is offered, both sides should be happy.

6

Making It Work

Showing Up The First Time

In order to get the benefits out of working with builders and helping them to sell their new homes to your customers, you must actually take people to see what the builders are offering.

The first step usually is identifying builders in your immediate market area that you think you might like to work with or "partner" with because of their location, reputation, price point, or product.

Then, you'll research them online and arrange to "preview" their operation to learn firsthand what is being offered and how you think you and your customers might like working with them.

Remember there is no requirement that you work with any particular builder or any certain number so identify and select only those builders that you are the most comfortable with.

This way when you do show up with your customers, you'll be able to focus on letting them enjoy the experience of finding a home that works for them rather than on determining how much you like the builder.

Now that you have met the builders in your market area that you want to work with and that you think have something beneficial to offer your customers, it's time for that first customer visit.

Recording Your Visit

When you arrive at the builder's location — a model home or new home sales center — with your customers, you'll want to register them to protect yourself and record the visit.

Even if you are not asked to do so, you'll want to make sure that you register yourself as the one responsible for bringing your customers. Then when a sale happens, there will be no question that you were the procuring agent.

This broker registration is in addition to the typical registration that your customers might need to complete on the builder's information card or visitor survey.

It may seem like just more paperwork, but this actually helps you in several ways.

Don't dismiss it or figure that you can do it on the next visit.

First, each time you visit with a new customer it establishes the fact that this is your customer and that you are the one responsible for introducing this customer to the builder.

This will help avoid any confusion later about who was the procuring cause.

Second, it provides a specified protection period for the registration to be in effect (and usually provides the terms and conditions for extending that registration period).

Finally, it confirms the amount of compensation and method of payment and makes sure that the builder has a way to contact you and your customers after the visit.

This becomes an enforceable agreement between you and the builder.

Registering Your Customers

Since this step is such an important one for linking you with your customers, you can plan ahead and be prepared to share your customer's contact information with the builder before you even arrive at their model or sales center.

Start by getting the correct spelling of your customer's name (or names) and their contact information and have it already written down — before you walk into the builder's office.

When you don't have to ask your customer for this information while you are in the sales center, you will look more prepared and in control — and professional.

Setting Yourself Apart

A great way to introduce your customers to whoever requests the registration information (the builder, the builder's representative, or a receptionist) is to have your customer's contact information already prepared before you arrive.

Use the back of your business card or an imprinted "Post-It" note (with your name and contact information on it) to jot down this information — which is a great reason for not printing anything on the back of your cards. You can also use a separate note sheet imprinted with your personal contact information.

You could even have some of your business cards printed with lines for this information on the backside of the cards where you could fill-in the information for your customers.

You also could have the builder's registration forms (which you got during your "preview" visit) filled out in advance.

Write down the name or names of your customers, their mailing address (preferably a temporary local one as well, if this is a relocation or purchase of a seasonal home), at least one email address for each adult in the customer group, and cellphone numbers.

Other information may be requested as well, but these are the essentials.

This will speed up the registration process, help set you apart from other Realtors® as being prepared, knowledgeable, and professional — and it will make the relationship with your customer look stronger.

This way it doesn't look like you just met your customers for the first time in the parking lot prior to entering the sales office — even if this was the first time actually seeing each other in-person.

"Partnering" With The Builder

"Partnering" may seem like a strange concept — especially when working with builders.

Think of it as a working relationship or a strategic alliance. That's what the term "partnering" means here — there are no binding legal relationships.

Essentially you and the builder are joining together on a case-by-case, as-needed basis, once or more than once, to serve the needs of your customers — in effect becoming temporary, ad hoc, non-binding, informal, strategic, transactional partners for that specific potential sale.

Both you and the builder you have selected want to find a home for your customers that meets their needs and their budget — and you have decided to work together to make this happen.

Obviously this is a business relationship, so you need to be comfortable that the builder you select to work with and "partner" with will respect your role and participation in any sale that occurs and pay you for producing the customer involved in that sale.

This is a conscious business decision by you.

Being Comfortable With The Builder

If you have any doubts or concerns about any builder you are considering working with about being paid after the sale is funded, getting paid on time, honoring their commitments to you and your customers, or delivering a finished home to your customers with no defects (or none that can't be easily and happily remedied), go someplace else with your customers. This is another reason for a preview visit.

Make sure you are comfortable with the ability of the builder to deliver what is promised, and take a look at the satisfaction level from previous purchasers and other Realtors®.

Before creating the relationship, actually talk to people who have worked with this builder.

They're Still Your Customers

When you work with a builder to help you produce a sale with your customers, you are not relinquishing control of your customers. Rather you are "lending" those customers to the builders to create a mutually beneficial transaction.

You need to be able to trust the builders or their representatives to work with you and your customers in a way that respects your customers and makes you look good in the eyes of your customers at the same time.

Again, this is why you should do your homework before taking anyone to work with a particular builder.

They should help you look credible and knowledgeable to your customers. After all, they are still your customers.

You are the one who generated those customers. How they got to you or learned about you is not important, just the fact that they are working with you.

When you appear at the builder's model center with customers that you produced, there is no question that they are working with you.

If you have spent the time to identify a trustworthy builder in advance of taking your customers there, you should not be concerned that they will try to separate you from your customers or discuss other properties. They should just be trying to make a sale with you.

That's how they make their money so there should be no hidden agendas or anything else going on except doing their best to help your customers identify and select a property from them.

Put your mind at ease. If there ever is an issue, then choose not to work with that builder anymore.

However, to make the sale and to process it after the sale is made, the builders or their representatives need the ability and the flexibility of contacting your customers directly (but usually with your knowledge) throughout the entire sales process to answer their questions, help them make a decision on a new home, and get it ready for closing and occupancy — so you can be paid.

It's Not A Contest

Remember your goal or objective in showing properties to people is to make a sale.

In working with a builder, you are relying on the builders or their representatives to help you make the sale.

The builders understand your relationship with your customers.

Therefore, it is not a contest between you and the builders to see who can sell your customers a home or who can be the most influential in persuading them to make the actual decision.

No points or trophies are awarded to the person making the sale. The real prize is the sale itself.

The reason you choose to work with or "partner" with a builder is because the homes they offer appeal to your customers.

Thus, trust the builders to help you make a sale and rely on their expertise about what they offer to help make your customers comfortable enough with what is available to want to make a purchasing decision.

Letting The Builder Help You

Both you and the builder that you're visiting have the same goal, and that is to help you make a sale to your customers.

Don't read anything into or confuse how they attempt to work with your customers — if they seem to be talking directly to your customers instead of always trying to include you in the discussion.

They just want to be able to do all that they can to make a sale (for and with you) as they work with your customers, answer their questions (while they are onsite and after they go home), show them what's available, maintain their excitement level, and help them identify a specific home that they can decide on to purchase and move into.

Allow the builder the freedom and professionalism to help you look good with your customers and to help you make a sale.

This is strictly an issue of letting each of you do what you're the best at.

You're the one who produces — and retains — your customers (the potential purchasers of what the builder is offering).

The builders and their staffs are responsible for working with your customers throughout the sales process to help make a sale happen so that you make money, your customers get a new home that meets their needs, and the builders make money as well.

Time Management Benefits

Deciding to work with a builder to show and sell a new home to your customers is a great way for you to use your time.

It's quite efficient.

The builder you select, or their team, will manage the entire sales process for you — from showing and explaining the opportunities available, helping you and your customers identify which one they would like to own that meets all of their criteria, doing the paperwork, processing the sale, facilitating the closing of title, and helping them get settled in their new home.

All the while, you have the freedom to pursue other aspects of your business, including working with additional customers or developing other aspects of your business.

Consider any builder or the builder's team that you choose to work with as your unpaid joint venture partner who performs all the day-to-day activities of working with your customers (with your full knowledge) to help them make a decision and then processing the sale so it will close.

This really is a time management benefit for you.

7

Adding Value To The Relationship

Helping Builders In Another Way

In addition to working with a builder to make a sale with one of your customers, another great opportunity for you to participate with builders is by helping them when they have other customers who need to sell their current home as a necessary condition of purchasing their new home.

Builders need capable, trustworthy, experienced Realtors® to help them accomplish this very important transaction — in a very timely way — and you can be a valuable resource for them. They need to be able to work with someone they can count on.

This is very important for the builders, and this is a very real opportunity for you.

You can perform a real service for builders that you are "partnering" with and get a free listing at the same time. Use it as a pocket listing or promote it on the MLS or your social media sites. The important thing is to get it sold — and sold quickly.

Homes To Sell Are A Big Issue

An issue that many builders face — and wished that they didn't have to — is working with people with a home to sell before they can purchase a brand new home from them.

In markets with several short sales and foreclosures, the issue may be even more pronounced as people have trouble getting what they want for their current home or what they need to have in order to proceed with the purchase of their new home.

When people who aren't working with a Realtor® come into a builder's model center — and they have a home to sell before they can finalize purchase of a new home from that builder — builders need and are looking for a way to help their would-be purchasers eliminate the condition that is preventing them from going ahead with the purchasing decision.

They need these homes sold, and they need to have it happen quickly.

Builders Need Current Homes Sold

Some people have already listed their homes with a Realtor® before visiting a builder's model center, and others are trying to sell their homes themselves (to save money).

Most are waiting until they find something they like before putting their homes on the market.

Regardless, builders need for their customers who have a current home standing in the way of them buying their new home to be able to sell their present homes as quickly as possible.

They would love to have a guarantee that people could sell their present homes within a month. That way they could go ahead and begin processing the sale with some degree of confidence that the current home was going to be a non-issue very quickly.

Therefore, builders need to be able to turn to someone like you that they know can price the existing homes correctly for a quick sale (without giving it away) so that they can make a sale and eliminate home-to-sell contingencies or delays.

Remember that most builders do not maintain a realty function separate from their new home sales. Thus, they have no way to assist their customers on their own to market their current properties.

When they have a customer that needs to sell their present home before going ahead with the purchase of a new one, those customers either have to sell it themselves or have a Realtor® help them.

So, why shouldn't you be the Realtor® who gets the job done?

You can help the builders' customers, make money, and become a reliable resource for the builders.

Becoming A Trusted Resource

Builders need a professional to turn to when they need help with a customer who has their current home to sell as a condition of purchasing a new home.

When people will not — or cannot — go ahead with the purchase of their home until their existing home is sold, builders need someone like you to get involved and help.

They need a resource like you to step in when they have a pending sale from a customer who has visited their model as a result of their website, newspaper advertising, signage, or some other means not involving another Realtor®. That customer needs to sell their present home (and sell it quickly at a realistic price) in order to be able to acquire the new home that they want from that builder.

By becoming a trusted resource for builders to rely on when they have customers who need to sell their existing home in order to proceed with buying their new home, you will receive several additional free listings and have the opportunity to make additional money while helping the builders at the same time.

This is a great way to cement your relationship with builders and a way to enhance your revenue as well.

Builders will essentially insist that people use you.

They know what you can do and will recommend that their buyers with a home to sell list their homes with you (or a couple of other Realtors® who have a similar reputation and relationship) in order to qualify for the builder's terms.

There's Plenty Of Upside For You

When you are selected — because of your expertise and ability — to help builders and their customers, this is an opportunity for everyone (and especially you) to do well.

First, you can help the builder make a sale who otherwise might not be able to retain his customers as potential purchasers — and ultimately close the sale — if there were no reasonable assurance that their present home could be sold quickly.

Second, you'll get to meet people in the process of selling your new listing who might need you to sell their home or help them find a new home in a different location.

You might even meet other Realtors® and develop a professional relationship with them when they view your listing or make a co-op sale with you on it.

Plus, you can get testimonials and potentially additional referrals from the seller, the people buying their home, and the builder.

Best of all, it's a free listing — the builder is giving it to you. All you have to do is meet with the customer and complete the listing agreement.

Establishing Your Reputation

Work on this ability to sell existing homes for builders. It has a big upside for you in terms of referrals, increased business, more visibility in your marketplace, and greater income opportunities.

Cultivate your relationship with the builders that you choose to work with — and with their on-site representatives as well.

You need for them to feel comfortable recommending you (either just you, or you and a couple of other Realtors® like you) to a potential purchaser as someone who is knowledgeable, professional, and capable of a successful and quick sale of their existing home.

It doesn't matter whether another Realtor® has tried to sell it for them in the past, if the listing is about to expire, if they've tried to sell it themselves, or it's a brand new opportunity that hasn't been on the market.

The appearance and condition of the home (interior and exterior), the curb appeal, the pricing, and the marketing could all be factors in why the home hasn't sold.

Earn the reputation with the builders that you choose to work with that you can help them in these instances by selling the existing homes of their customers quickly.

You will become an invaluable asset for them and become a "go-to" resource to help them.

A Different Type Of "Partnering"

Just as you "partner" with a builder to show their homes to your customers, now they can "partner" with you.

They are selecting your expertise and ability to help their potential purchasers achieve a quick sale of their current homes — necessary for them to proceed with acquiring their new one from the builder.

Based on your reputation and ability, the builder may even feel comfortable enough to grant the customer a "home-to-sell" contingency on the purchase of their new home, knowing that you can sell their existing home quickly.

Work toward establishing yourself as such a resourceful professional who can accomplish this.

Performance Is What Counts

Initially builders might choose to work with you because of what you promise, because of the number of sales you have produced with them, or because they like you.

For a continuing relationship, however, builders need to experience results.

It's all based on performance.

The reason that builders will select you to market existing homes for their purchasers is because you can get the job done.

Other factors might be important, but making the sale — and doing it quickly — is the main thing that matters.

Earning The Builders' Trust

Trust needs to work both ways in any healthy relationship.

Just remember that when the builders or their representatives call on you to help out with one of their customers that they are expecting you to help sell the customer's current home and nothing more (such as trying to interest them in a different property).

This is the same way that you trust the builders or their onsite sales representatives to respect the relationship that you have with any customer that you have produced by not trying to discuss any other properties with them or sell them anything but the homes that the builders have for sale — already built or to-be-built.

When such relationships between you and the builders or their onsite sales representatives work as they are designed, everyone wins — you, the customers, and the builders.

As a result, you will have developed an additional income opportunity from working with builders and will have strengthened your referral potential (from both the builder and the customers).

This is another great way to work with builders.

8

More Ways To Benefit

Exploring Other Relationships

Mostly we have been looking at how to work with builders and make money — by taking your customers to a builder and "partnering" with them to make a sale or by listing and selling an existing home for one of the builders' purchasers.

There are other ways to work with builders that don't involve being paid but still have a benefit for you and your business.

Most of them involve no pay so they could be considered as non-cash opportunities, but some could generate some consideration in the form of special recognition, dinners, awards, and small cash prizes or incentives.

So instead of non-cash, let's call them non-sales opportunities. They may result from sales activities, but remuneration will not be based on specific transactions or the amount of the sale.

Non-Sales Opportunities

Working with builders and establishing relationships with them to show and sell their new homes to your customers can have additional benefits besides just getting paid a commission for making a sale.

It can put you on an inside track to learning about what the builder is planning and designing and in participating in the marketing of new products.

Builders often use Realtors® that they know and respect as sounding boards for new ideas.

In short, you can become a trusted ally of builders — one or more than one — based on your willingness to help them when asked for your opinions and your professionalism in working with them to make sales.

Special Sales Opportunities

Occasionally, because of the relationships you're creating with builders, you might be contacted and invited to participate in special sales opportunities —

almost exclusive ones — to help builders and their representatives sell specific homes or make sales goals at the end of a month or quarter.

There might be certain inventory homes that need to be sold, and you might be given a special financial incentive, spiff, or bonus for producing a buyer.

Maybe it's just a case of helping builders reach a sales goal or quota for the month and qualifying for a spiff or bonus for helping them achieve it.

By showing that you are willing to work with builders and that you understand the new home sales process, you'll receive a special invitation to participate while other Realtors® will just hear about opportunities through normal channels.

You will have preferred status.

Staying In The Know

By being part of the preferred network, you may receive special emails or have access to a private webpage on builders' websites.

While builders and their staffs will send out eblasts, text messages, fax blasts, and flyers, or post new content or updates on their social media or web pages to Realtors® in general, you will receive the premium edition of such notifications — maybe before the others do, maybe with special incentives, and maybe with more details.

Being selected to be on the premium mailing or notification list isn't automatic just because you show an interest in builders' products or produce a sale now and then — and it's not something you can request.

You have to be contacted and invited to be part of a premium or preferred group, Realtors® Council, or similar group that various builders establish.

Many new home salespeople create their own groups as well.

Inside Track

When you are invited to be part of any builder's preferred Realtor® group, Realtors® Council, or any group such as this — regardless of its name — you'll want to accept.

You will get earlier or more complete email notifications about pending changes in pricing or terms, availability or certain homes, special spiffs or financing that might be offered, new products, or limited time promotions.

There might be occasional breakfasts or lunches where you'll be invited to attend to share information on your experiences in the marketplace and to hear about what those builders are planning.

Builders might be interested in making your experiences in working with them even more beneficial for all parties involved.

Feedback and Focus Groups

As builders develop new products or tweak their existing ones, as they look for new advertising campaigns to attract customers to look at their homes, as they look for competitive pricing strategies, as they try to appeal to what Realtors® want to see in a new home or community for their customers, as they determine what features to include in the price of their homes and which ones to offer as options, and many other items concerning their sales, marketing, construction, and customer relations, they are going to want the opinions of Realtors® as well as consumers.

Since you'll have a relationship with them and are active in the area, builders will want to include you in their focus groups, informal sounding boards, and independent surveys. This gives you an opportunity to share your honest and professional opinions — and to make the experience of shopping for and selecting a new home that much more pleasant for you and your customers.

There might even be a small cash thank-you gift or other gratuity for participating.

Awards And Recognition

Finally, working with builders and doing such a good job that they want to award or recognize you, is a great way to profit professionally, if not financially.

You might receive a plaque, trophy, club membership, auto lease, trip, or some other type of prize.

You might find your picture and success story on their web pages, blogs, or newsletters.

Doing a good job for your customers and "partnering" with a builder can be its own reward, but there are many other ways that a relationship with builders can be worthwhile.

9

Final Thoughts

Your Business Is Sales

While both you and the builders have service aspects to your businesses, essentially both of you are sales organizations.

Maintain the focus.

The builder wants to make sales, and you want to make sales.

This is why you will have "partnered" with a builder by taking your customers to their model center in the hopes of having a sale occur.

Therefore, when your customers that you have taken to a particular builder's model center seem interested in a particular home well enough to invest in it and live in it, you have succeeded.

You have brought buyer and seller together for a sale to occur.

It's not a requirement that your customers be shown a certain number or variety of homes before they are ready to make a decision on their new home.

When they are ready to purchase, you are ready.

Just keep the end game in mind — making a sale.

The Customer's Opinion Counts

It's very important that you verify that any builder that you decide to "partner" with has products that you can enthusiastically recommend — even if they don't match your personal tastes.

Even if you would not buy homes that you are showing your customers because of the price point or the layout not meeting your particular needs, assure yourself that the builder delivers a quality product that is worthy of your customer's investment if and when they like the product for themselves and their needs.

There could be other homes somewhere — either new homes or resales — that could eventually satisfy the needs of your customers, but encourage your customers to make a decision if they like what they have seen and seem ready to go ahead.

The Search Is Over

When your customers decide on a new home and want to go ahead and complete the paperwork, step back and let the sales proceed.

There is no reason that your customers can't make a decision to buy on the first day, at the first community, or with the first home that you show them if it's really something that appeals to them.

If they really seem to like a home you have shown them, and it meets their needs, all of the other properties that you thought they should see and consider become irrelevant.

It's time to enjoy your sale with them.

Even if there were other properties that you had intended to show your customers — or ones that you had shown and planned on visiting with them again if they didn't want to make their decision on what they were seeing there — this no longer matters when the decision to buy a particular builder's home has been made and you have succeeded in helping your customers come to that decision.

Remember that it does not matter whether or not you personally like the style or layout of a particular new home as long as your customers do — and as long as you truly believe that your customers are getting good value for their investment and that it addresses the needs that they expressed.

Again, this is why it's so important to do your research and your homework before you take your customers to see what builders offer. You need to make sure that you can endorse it and support your customers' decision to purchase there.

The Builders Process The Sale

Once the decision has been made by your customers, it's time to let the builders take over and have the rest of the sales process run its course.

From this point forward, the builders will complete and attend to all of the details of getting the paperwork prepared, notices filed, inspections completed, applications filed and approved, and legalities completed for the sale to close.

Of course, they will also work with your customers as necessary to get them approved by their lender.

This takes so many of the details off your plate.

The time management and allocation benefits that accrue to you by "partnering" with a builder are tremendous when it comes to getting the sale on paper and getting it to the closing table.

Staying Informed

Just make sure that you have selected to work with builders who will keep both you and your customers informed of everything that is required and when it is needed. You want your customers to enjoy this experience.

You need to know how all the paperwork and procedures are progressing toward completion and the updated status for finishing their new home.

Insist that the builders keep you up-to-date on everything connected to getting your customers approved and getting their new home completed and ready for occupancy.

This includes conversations and correspondence with official parties involved in approving various aspects of the sale.

You should never feel excluded from anything going on in the new home sales process or feel that anything mysterious is happening.

You should be kept informed of what is happening at every stage. Neither you nor your customer should have questions that go unanswered or anything that you can't ask about and receive an answer.

Builders Want To Work With You

Most builders recognize that you are a significant source of producing high quality customers. They want your business, and they value your participation.

Find those builders that recognize your value in "partnering" with them to produce sales and work with them.

Remember that working with builders to sell their products to your customers is a fantastic way to improve your bottom line while satisfying the needs of your customers and being extremely efficient.

Steve Hoffacker

Steve Hoffacker, CAPS, MCSP, MIRM, is the manager at Hoffacker Associates LLC, a sales training (new home sales, universal design, and aging-in-place) and coaching company based in West Palm Beach, Florida.

Steve is an award-winning, internationally-recognized and experienced new home salesperson and sales trainer, as well as a universal design/aging-in-place safety and accessibility sales trainer and instructor.

For more than 30 years, he has helped homebuilders, new home salespeople, contractors and remodelers, new home marketers, designers, architects, occupational therapists, Realtors®, and other professionals to be more visible, competitive, profitable, and effective — and to really enjoy themselves as they pursue their business and create wonderful customer experiences.

Steve wants you and your company to be successful and has created this and many other books to help make that happen.

This book will be a great resource to help you take your business to another level and outpace the competition.

Use these strategies and concepts for your professional success.

www.ingramcontent.com/pod-product-compliance
Lightning Source LLC
Chambersburg PA
CBHW071208200326
41519CB00018B/5428